LEFT OUT
OF HISTORY

THe ReaL HisTORY OF
THANKSGIVING

Cayla Bellanger DeGroat
Cicely Lewis, Executive Editor

Lerner Publications ◆ Minneapolis

LETTER FROM CICELY LEWIS

CICELY LEWIS

Dear Reader,

It has been said that if we do not learn from our history, we will make the same mistakes. Yet what happens when stories from history are missing, buried, or told from a single viewpoint?

This series sheds light on stories that have been left out of history. As you flip through the pages, you may hear new perspectives you have not heard before. Ask yourself: Who is telling the story? What is their perspective? Why does it matter?

The Read Woke challenge invites readers to question the status quo. I want my students to read books that confront traditional narratives and share stories from underrepresented and oppressed groups. I created Read Woke Books because I want you to be informed and compassionate citizens.

Power to the Reader,

—Cicely Lewis, Executive Editor

TABLE OF CONTENTS

Think critically about the photos and illustrations throughout this book. Who is taking the photos or creating the illustrations? What viewpoint do they represent? How does this affect your viewpoint?

In the Spirit of Metacom

NATIONAL DAY OF MOURNING
UNITED AMERICAN INDIANS OF NEW ENGLAND

NOT EVERYONE CELEBRATES THANKSGIVING

What do you picture when you think of Thanksgiving? Is it relatives from near and far gathering around the family table, set with turkey, stuffing, cranberries, mashed potatoes, and pumpkin pie? Is it watching a parade or a football game on television? Is it something else?

Now imagine spending Thanksgiving in Plymouth, Massachusetts. It's noon and the Atlantic Ocean is dazzling in the distance. The sun provides warmth in the autumn chill. The sweet smell of burning sage wafts over you, and you

People pray during the National Day of Mourning in 2007.

listen intently as an elder says a prayer. You are observing the National Day of Mourning.

This yearly event occurs on Thanksgiving Day. The National Day of Mourning honors the lives of Native American ancestors, acknowledges the real history of Thanksgiving, and highlights issues that impact Indigenous communities.

Both Thanksgiving and the National Day of Mourning have roots in America's past. Holding these celebrations on the same day shows that Thanksgiving holds different meanings for everyone.

An 1848 painting by British painter Charles Lucy showing Pilgrims landing in Massachusetts

CHaPTer 1
THE SAINTS AND THE WAMPANOAG

THE STORY OF THANKSGIVING USUALLY BEGINS WITH ENGLISH IMMIGRANTS, COMMONLY CALLED THE PILGRIMS, AND THEIR TREK ACROSS THE ATLANTIC OCEAN ON THE *MAYFLOWER.* They landed in present-day Massachusetts in the late fall of 1620 and created a settlement called Plymouth Colony. The pilgrims called themselves "Saints."

A reproduction of a historic Wampanoag home, which is called a wetu

Long before the Pilgrims arrived, Indigenous tribes occupied the North Atlantic Coast of North America. These tribes had lived there for many generations in prosperous towns and villages. They were farmers who grew crops such as corn, beans, and squash. Each of these tribes has its own language, culture, and government. When the Pilgrims arrived, they built Plymouth Colony on Wampanoag land.

In the spring of 1621, two Wampanoag sachems, or leaders, Massasoit and Samoset, met with the Pilgrims. Their goal was to create an alliance. Between 1616 and 1619, up to 90 percent of the Indigenous population in the Plymouth region died from European diseases. The many deaths in their tribe weakened the Wampanoag, and tensions between the

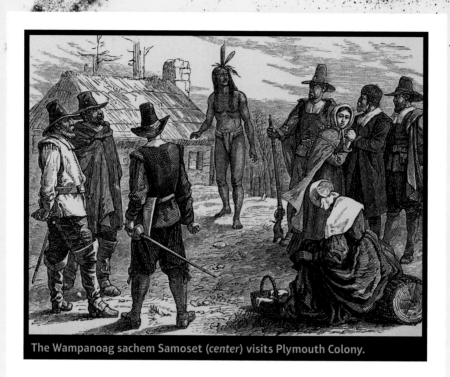

The Wampanoag sachem Samoset (*center*) visits Plymouth Colony.

Wampanoag and the Narragansett were rising. Tisquantum, a member of the Patuxet, a band of the Wampanoag, translated during the meeting.

The Pilgrims were also in desperate need of allies. They were in foreign lands and lacked the necessary food, resources, and knowledge to survive. Nearly half the Pilgrims died from illness during their first winter in Plymouth. Those who survived lived by stealing from the graves and

DiD YOU KNOW?

The Pilgrims were not the first group of Europeans to arrive in North America and meet with Indigenous tribes. Other Europeans had already been invading the lands for over one hundred years.

The Vikings were from Scandinavia, a region in northern Europe, and came to North America over one thousand years ago. The Vikings were some of the first Europeans to arrive in North America.

REFLECT

Historians have limited information and differing opinions about Tisquantum. The information we have comes from the accounts of Europeans and Pilgrims. Why is it important to know who is telling Tisquantum's story? How might his story be influenced by their perspective? What might be missing?

An illustration depicting Tisquantum (*right*) helping a Pilgrim

Massasoit (*front center*) and other Wampanoag met with Pilgrims at Plymouth Colony in 1621.

winter food storage of a Wampanoag village.

At the meeting, the Wampanoag and Pilgrims worked out a treaty of peace and mutual protection.

DiD YOU KNOW?

Some estimates put the population of the entire Wampanoag confederation prior to 1619 at more than one hundred thousand people. They had sixty-nine villages and lived in present-day southeastern Massachusetts and eastern Rhode Island.

TISQUANTUM

WHO WAS HE?

- Known also as Squanto

- Was a Native American interpreter, guide, and liaison

CHILDHOOD AND SLAVERY

- Believed to have been born sometime in the late 1500s

- Born into the Patuxet, part of the Wampanoag confederation who lived on lands in present-day Massachusetts and Rhode Island

- Was kidnapped as a child by European enslavers and sold into slavery in Europe

- Learned to speak English while enslaved

RETURNING HOME

- Escaped slavery and returned home sometime in 1619

- Discovered he was the only survivor among an estimated two thousand Patuxet who had died from diseases brought by European settlers

AN IMPORTANT LIAISON

- Lived among the Wampanoag people after returning home

- Became an interpreter between the Wampanoag and the Pilgrim settlement of Plymouth in 1621 and helped maintain peace between them

- Taught Pilgrims of Plymouth Colony agricultural methods and helped them establish trade relations, critical to their survival

- Died in November 1622

American painter Jean Leon Gerome Ferris's oil painting of the first Thanksgiving

CHapter 2
NO THANKS, NO GIVING

HISTORIANS DEBATE WHAT THE FIRST THANKSGIVING LOOKED LIKE AND WHETHER IT WAS PLANNED. This is because few primary sources on the history of the event exist. The history of Thanksgiving is also often missing Native American perspectives.

Two written accounts are from Pilgrims about the event that we now think of as the first Thanksgiving. Leaders of

Plymouth Colony, Edward Winslow and William Bradford, wrote them. In *Mourt's Relation*, Winslow describes a gathering after the colonists had finished their harvest. A group of ninety Wampanoag, including Massasoit, joined them for a three-day event. Winslow wrote that the Saints survived by the grace and goodness of God, not crediting the Wampanoag for their help.

In *Of Plimoth Plantation*, Bradford details the settlers' harvest of that year, including a mention of wild turkeys. Neither Winslow's nor Bradford's account mentions "thanks" or "Thanksgiving." Following this Thanksgiving, Indigenous peoples suffered from loss of land, war, death, and disease.

In 1620 William Bradford and other men sign the Mayflower Compact, the first governmental document to be used in what became the US.

Europeans exposed the Wampanoag and other Native American nations to diseases such as smallpox. The variola virus (*shown here*) causes smallpox.

After 1621, relations between the Pilgrims and the Wampanoag grew tense, and disagreements erupted between Tisquantum and Massasoit. European diseases continued to spread among Indigenous peoples, causing illness and death.

REFLECT

Think about where our information on Thanksgiving comes from. Why is it important to learn more about sources of information?

An engraved portrait of Metacom, a leader of the Wampanoag

"People need to understand that you need to be thankful each and every day—that was how our ancestors thought and navigated this world. Because we were thankful, we were willing to share . . . and we had good intentions and a good heart."

—BRIAN MOSKWETAH WEEDEN,
chairperson of the Mashpee Wampanoag Tribe, in November 2021

After Massasoit's death around 1661, his sons Wamsutta and Metacom (known to the English as King Philip) led the Wampanoag. They continued their alliance with the Pilgrims, but relations between the groups worsened because the Pilgrims pushed for more land. War broke out in 1675. King Philip's War is considered to be the most violent, devastating war fought on American land.

In 1637 Massachusetts Bay Colony held a day of thanksgiving after killing many members of the Pequot tribe. The Pequot lived on. Here, chairperson of the Mashantucket Pequot Tribal Nation Rodney Butler celebrates during Schemitzun, the Green Corn Festival, in 2021.

CHAPTER 3
AN AMERICAN HOLIDAY MYTH

OVER THE NEXT FEW HUNDRED YEARS, THERE WERE MANY DAYS OF THANKSGIVING, BUT THANKSGIVING WAS STILL NOT A HOLIDAY. In 1637 Governor John Winthrop of the Massachusetts Bay Colony had a day of thanksgiving to celebrate the return of their men from a battle against the

Pequot tribe at Mystic, Connecticut. That battle devastated the Pequot. Over seven hundred men, women, and children were enslaved and massacred, giving this day of thanksgiving a grim meaning.

In 1863 President Abraham Lincoln created an official Thanksgiving holiday for the last Thursday in November. This was the start of celebrating Thanksgiving each year.

In 1941 the US Congress wanted to set a fixed date for Thanksgiving. In some years, November has four Thursdays, and in other years, it has five. Congress chose the fourth Thursday in November to be the official day of Thanksgiving.

Americans celebrate Thanksgiving by having dinner together in 1940.

The Macy's Thanksgiving Day Parade started in 1924. Many people watch the parade every year, including this parade from 1940.

Native American perspectives often have been left out of the teachings about Thanksgiving. How does learning about history from multiple points of view improve your understanding of historical events and humanity?

Thanksgiving traditions expanded to include entertainment and community recreation. Common features included community parades, turkey shoots, and football games. During this time, imagery of painted, feathered Indians and buckle-hat Pilgrims became familiar.

Millions of people in the US celebrate Thanksgiving.

Native Americans attend the Mashpee Wampanoag Powwow on July 6, 2013. The event includes contests, drumming, and dancing.

CHAPTER 4
BEYOND THANKSGIVING

IN 1970 THE MASSACHUSETTS DEPARTMENT OF COMMERCE PREPARED TO CELEBRATE THE 350TH ANNIVERSARY OF THE FIRST THANKSGIVING BY HOLDING A BANQUET IN PLYMOUTH, MASSACHUSETTS. They invited Wamsutta Frank James, an activist and member of the Wampanoag Tribe of

Gay Head Aquinnah, to give a speech. But his speech included a more complicated version of Thanksgiving. It described the myths of the holiday and how it hid the dark truth of the pain Native Americans have suffered since the holiday's beginning. The Massachusetts Department of Commerce forbid James from giving the speech.

"And so down through the years there is record after record of Indian lands taken and, in token, reservations set up for him upon which to live. The Indian, having been stripped of his power, could only stand by and watch while the white man took his land and used it for his personal gain. This the Indian could not understand; for to him, land was survival, to farm, to hunt, to be enjoyed. It was not to be abused."

—WAMSUTTA FRANK JAMES,
excerpt from his suppressed speech

DiD YOU KNOW?

Each year, the National Day of Mourning observances include a feast that feeds up to five hundred people. The observances also include prayer, reflection, speeches from elders, and a march from Plymouth Rock to downtown Plymouth.

On November 25, 2021, Chali'naru Dones (*front*), a Taíno-Boricua woman, participates in a march for the National Day of Mourning.

REFLECT

Think about how stories of our ancestors influence our perceptions of the world. What stories have shaped how you see the world?

James's rejection from the banquet became the start of the National Day of Mourning for Native Americans. Ceremonies for the National Day of Mourning are organized by the United American Indians of New England, a group that works to bust the myths of Thanksgiving and shed light on the harms that racism and colonization have done to Indigenous peoples and nations.

The real history of Thanksgiving shows that Indigenous peoples have been shaping North America for many generations. Indigenous knowledge and values were vital to the survival of the Pilgrims four hundred years ago and continue to be relevant. Their knowledge, culture, and histories are embedded in the fabric of the United States' past, present, and future.

CONNECT AND REFLECT

Consider the way this book tells the story of Thanksgiving. Think about an important event in your life. How would you tell a friend about it? How might that story be different if another person told it? Why is it important who tells a story?

Chali'naru Dones

GLOSSARY

ALLIANCE: when groups of people agree to work together toward a common goal

ANCESTOR: a person from whom someone is descended

COLONY: an area where a group of people settle that stays under control of their home country

MASSACRE: killing a large number of people in a cruel or violent way

PERSPECTIVE: a specific point of view

PRIMARY SOURCE: a direct, firsthand account of an event

PROSPEROUS: successful or wealthy

SACHEM: a North American Indian chief, especially the chief of a confederation of the Algonquian tribes of the North Atlantic Coast

TREATY: an agreement between two or more groups of people

SOURCE NOTES

18   Associated Press, "Native American Tribes Are Gathering in
      Plymouth to Mourn on Thanksgiving," NPR, November 25, 2021,
      https://www.npr.org/2021/11/25/1059212893/native-american
      -tribes-are-gathering-in-plymouth-to-mourn-on-thanksgiving
      #:~:text=Native%20American%20tribes%20are%20gathering
      %20in%20Plymouth%20to%20mourn%20on%20Thanksgiving.

24   Wamsutta Frank James, "The Suppressed Speech of Wamsutta
      (Frank B.) James, Wampanoag," September 10, 1970, available
      online at UAINE, http://www.uaine.org/suppressed_speech.htm.

READ WOKE READING LIST

Keene, Adrienne. *Notable Native People: 50 Indigenous Leaders, Dreamers, and Changemakers from Past and Present*. Emeryville, CA: Ten Speed, 2021.

Mashpee Wampanoag Tribe: Timeline
https://mashpeewampanoagtribe-nsn.gov/timeline

National Museum of the American Indian
https://americanindian.si.edu

Native Americans
https://kids.nationalgeographic.com/history/topic/native -americans

Newell, Chris. *If You Lived during the Plimoth Thanksgiving*. New York: Scholastic, 2021.

Sorell, Traci. *We Are Still Here! Native American Truths Everyone Should Know*. Watertown, MA: Charlesbridge, 2021.

Treuer, Anton. *Everything You Wanted to Know about Indians but Were Afraid to Ask*. Young Readers Edition. Montclair, NJ: Levine Querido, 2021.

United American Indians of New England
http://www.uaine.org

INDEX

PHOTO ACKNOWLEDGMENTS

Image credits: BRYAN R. SMITH/AFP/Getty Images, p. 4; AP Photo/Lisa Poole, p. 5; Photography Collection, Miriam and Ira D. Wallach Division of Art, Prints and Photographs, The New York Public Library, p. 6; Suchan/Getty Images, p. 7; Internet Archive Book Images/flickr (Public Domain), p. 8; Pictures from History/ Universal Images Group/Getty Images, p. 9; AF Fotografie/Alamy Stock Photo, p. 10; MPI/Getty Images, pp. 11, 15; Library of Congress, p. 14; Kateryna Kon/ Shutterstock, p. 16; Kean Collection/Getty Images, p. 17; AP Photo/Jessica Hill, p. 19; Bettmann/Getty Images, pp. 20, 21; Rawpixel.com/Shutterstock, p. 22; Essdras M Suarez/The Boston Globe/Getty Images, p. 23; Keiko Hiromi/AFLO/ Alamy Stock Photo, p. 25; Sue Dorfman/ZUMA Wire/Alamy Stock Photo, p. 27.

Design elements: Ursa Major/Shutterstock; Mint Images/Getty Images; Jose A. Bernat Bacete/Moment/Getty Images.

Cover images: Bryan R. Smith/AFP/Getty Images; Jessica Rinaldi/The Boston Globe/Getty Images.

Cecily Lewis portrait photos by Fernando Decillis.

To Jory and Ezra

Content consultant credit: Dr. Jill Doerfler

Lerner Publications Company
An imprint of Lerner Publishing Group, Inc.
241 First Avenue North
Minneapolis, MN 55401 USA

For reading levels and more information, look up this title at www.lernerbooks.com.

Main body text set in Aptifer Sans LT Pro.
Typeface provided by Linotype AG.

Editor: Brianna Kaiser **Designer:** Viet Chu
Lerner team: Martha Kranes

Library of Congress Cataloging-in-Publication Data

Names: Bellanger DeGroat, Cayla, author.
Title: The real history of Thanksgiving / Cayla Bellanger DeGroat.
Description: Minneapolis : Lerner Publications, [2023] | Series: Left out of history (read woke books) | Includes bibliographical references and index. | Audience: Ages 9–14 | Audience: Grades 4–6 | Summary: "Thanksgiving is a popular holiday in the United States. But many people don't know the true or whole history of the holiday. Readers will learn how Thanksgiving started and its lasting legacy in the U.S."— Provided by publisher.
Identifiers: LCCN 2022008723 (print) | LCCN 2022008724 (ebook) | ISBN 9781728475844 (lib. bdg.) | ISBN 9781728479101 (pbk.) | ISBN 9781728482941 (eb pdf)
Subjects: LCSH: Massachusetts—History—New Plymouth, 1620–1691—Juvenile literature. | Pilgrims (New Plymouth Colony)—Juvenile literature. | Wampanoag Indians—Juvenile literature. | Thanksgiving Day—History—Juvenile literature. | United States—History—Errors, inventions, etc.—Juvenile literature.
Classification: LCC F68 .D42 2023 (print) | LCC F68 (ebook) | DDC 973.2/2—dc23/eng/20220513

LC record available at https://lccn.loc.gov/2022008723
LC ebook record available at https://lccn.loc.gov/2022008724

Manufactured in the United States of America
1-52151-50614-8/2/2022